MODERN ROLE MODELS

David Beckham

Slade Media Center

Jim Whiting

Mason Crest Publishers

Produced by OTTN Publishing in association with
21st Century Publishing and Communications, Inc.

MASON CREST PUBLISHERS INC.
370 Reed Road
Broomall, Pennsylvania 19008
(866) MCP-BOOK (toll free)
www.masoncrest.com

Printed in the United States of America.

First Printing

9 8 7 6 5 4 3 2 1

Library of Congress Cataloging-in-Publication Data

Whiting, Jim, 1943–
    David Beckham / by Jim Whiting.
        p. cm. — (Modern role models)
    Includes bibliographical references.
ISBN-13: 978-1-4222-0480-1 (hardcover) — ISBN-13: 978-1-4222-0767-3 (pbk.)
ISBN-10: 1-4222-0480-4 (hardcover)
 1. Beckham, David, 1975–   —Juvenile literature. 2. Soccer players—England—Biography—Juvenile literature. I. Title.
GV942.7.B432W486 2009
796.334092—dc22
[B]   2008020407

Publisher's note:
All quotations in this book come from original sources, and contain the spelling and grammatical inconsistencies of the original text.

CROSS-CURRENTS

In the ebb and flow of the currents of life we are each influenced by many people, places, and events that we directly experience or have learned about. Throughout the chapters of this book you will come across *CROSS-CURRENTS* reference boxes. These boxes direct you to a *CROSS-CURRENTS* section in the back of the book that contains fascinating and informative sidebars and related pictures. Go on. ▶▶

CONTENTS

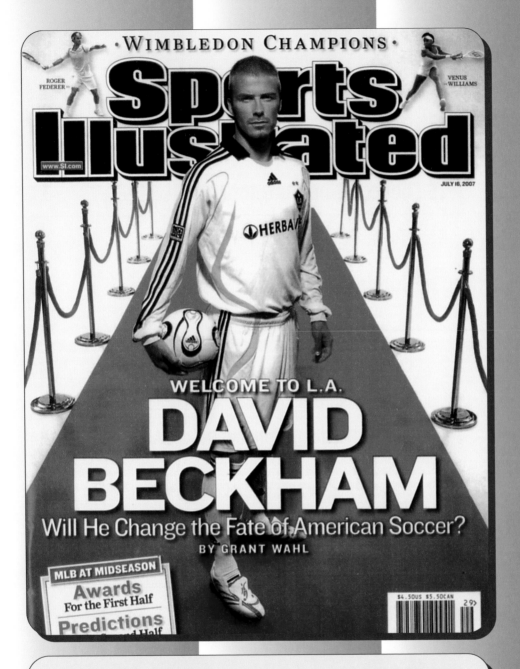

WIMBLEDON CHAMPIONS

Sports Illustrated

www.SI.com

ROGER FEDERER

VENUS WILLIAMS

JULY 16, 2007

HERBALIFE

WELCOME TO L.A.

DAVID BECKHAM

Will He Change the Fate of American Soccer?

BY GRANT WAHL

MLB AT MIDSEASON
Awards
For the First Half
Predictions

$4.50US $5.50CAN

David Beckham was featured on the cover of the July 2007 issue of *Sports Illustrated*—just one of many covers on which he appeared after signing a five-year contract with an American soccer team. The amazing deal would pay David $50 million a year to play for the Los Angeles Galaxy.

1

Welcome to Los Angeles

HOLLYWOOD PARTY HOSTS DON'T GET MUCH bigger than Tom Cruise, Katie Holmes, Will Smith, and Jada Pinkett Smith. Many movie and TV celebrities attended their July 2007 bash, but the guest of honor wasn't a film star, even though his name had appeared in the title of a hit 2002 film. It was English soccer superstar David Beckham.

No one—especially David himself—would say that he is the best soccer player of all time. Nor is he even the best player in recent years. But no one in the game has a higher public profile or broader appeal. Part of this appeal is due to his superlative soccer skills. Another part is because of the dramatic turns in his career. At times, he has caused controversy, drawn criticism, and even received death threats. Beckham's appeal also comes from the fact that he does many things off the field that contradict the macho image of soccer. He has cried openly, posed for underwear commercials, sponsored a line of men's colognes, contributed to charitable causes, and more.

Further raising David's public profile is his superstar wife, Victoria. Victoria was once known as Posh Spice, a member of the Spice Girls. Because of their combined fame, the Beckhams have one of the world's highest-profile marriages, and they are frequently targeted by **paparazzi**.

⋙ THE STARS COME OUT ⋘

Given this level of fame, the high turnout of Hollywood **glitterati** for an evening of dining, dancing, and rubbing shoulders with Posh and Beckham wasn't surprising. The guest list at the bash included Eva Longoria Parker, Demi Moore and Ashton Kutcher, Jim Carrey and Jenny McCarthy, Rihanna, and Queen Latifah. Singer Stevie Wonder even provided part of the evening's entertainment with a 15-minute set that included his hit "Signed, Sealed, Delivered."

That musical choice was especially appropriate, because a few months earlier Beckham had signed the biggest contract in the history of Major League Soccer (MLS), the leading professional league in the United States. He was going to earn $50 million a year for five years from the Los Angeles Galaxy. But he had been given a formidable task: to deliver performances that would raise the profile of professional soccer in the United States.

While soccer, or football, is probably the most popular sport in the rest of the world, it never caught on as a spectator sport in the United States. In the mid-1970s, the New York Cosmos of the North American Soccer League (NASL) signed Brazilian superstar Pelé in an effort to boost attendance. While Pelé's presence achieved that goal during his playing days, he soon retired, and the league folded in the 1980s.

CROSS-CURRENTS

For more information about the professional soccer league in the United States, check out "Major League Soccer." Go to page 48. ▶▶

⋙ A MINOR SPORT ⋘

The MLS was formed about a decade later, in the mid-1990s. Currently, there are 14 active teams, and expansion teams will soon begin play in Seattle and Philadelphia. Yet soccer attracts only a fraction of the fan and media attention of college and professional football and basketball and Major League Baseball.

Clearly, David has been given a difficult mission. As he told Grant Wahl of *Sports Illustrated*:

Because of their good looks and talent, David and his wife Victoria easily fit into the celebrity culture of Los Angeles. Here, Beckham (23) waves to his sons Cruz, Romeo, and Brooklyn. Victoria (wearing sunglasses) is seated, while friends Tom Cruise and Katie Holmes stand and cheer for the Galaxy star.

"I'm not silly enough to think I'm going to change the whole culture, because it's not going to happen, but I do have a belief that soccer can go to a different level, and I'd love to be a part of that."

David (front row, second from right) poses with his Los Angeles Galaxy teammates before his first start in a Major League Soccer match, August 15, 2007. David, who was named captain of the team, scored his first MLS goal on a free kick that day. He also assisted on his team's second goal as Los Angeles beat D.C. United, 2-0.

The reaction of soccer fans in Seattle suggests that Beckham's belief might be right. The team sold more than 3,000 season tickets in less than 24 hours when they went on sale. There's little doubt that the chance to see Beckham play against the Seattle Sounders was a factor.

It's also likely that David's introduction to the league comes at a better time than when Pelé tried to woo Americans to soccer stadiums. Simon Fuller, producer of *American Idol* and Beckham's manager, told Wahl:

CROSS-CURRENTS

If you would like to learn about one of the greatest soccer players of all time, read "Pelé." Go to page 48. ▶▶

❝There seems to be a real foundation now for soccer [in the U.S.]. David is the most iconic of all footballers, and he's achieved pretty much everything you can achieve in Europe, apart from maybe winning a big tournament with England. He's still in his early 30s, still playing remarkably well.❞

A young player in his prime, with fame already squarely on his side, may be just the thing to turn soccer from a minor sport into a major draw.

⟫ ON THE SIDELINES ⟪

David didn't play especially well in his Galaxy **debut** the day before the Hollywood party. In fact, he almost didn't play at all because he was suffering from an ankle injury. He spent most of the game on the sidelines, and the TV cameras and the crowd often seemed to be paying more attention to him than to the action on the field. He was cheered every time he stood up and stretched. He finally entered the game with less than 15 minutes remaining but didn't have any significant effect on the outcome. The Galaxy lost 1-0 to Chelsea, an English team. Afterward, he told reporters:

❝My 15 minutes, it was nice to get out there. I haven't trained all week. I hadn't kicked a ball yet today. It was just nice to be out there with the lads and get this game over and done with. I enjoyed it.❞

U.S. soccer officials hope that David's enjoyment is contagious. While he knows that he can't singlehandedly make soccer into one of America's most important sports, he believes that he can make a difference. And more than anything else, he remains thankful for the opportunity to make a living playing the game he loves.

Holding a soccer ball, David is photographed with his parents, Ted and Sandra Beckham, outside their home in the Leytonstone neighborhood of London, circa 1986. That year, David attended the Bobby Charlton Soccer School, where he was coached by one of England's greatest soccer players. At the end of the camp, the 11-year-old received the Bobby Charlton Soccer Skills Award.

Kid with the Golden Kick

DAVID WAS BORN TO TED AND SANDRA BECKHAM in the Leytonstone neighborhood of East London, England, on May 2, 1975. His dad worked as a gas fitter, while his mother was a hairdresser. David joined a sister, Lynne, who was three years older. Joanne would round out the family five years later.

Ted Beckham was a good amateur soccer player and a longtime fan of the Manchester United Red Devils. Affectionately known as United, it is probably the most famous soccer team in England. His affection likely influenced his son's early development.

⟫ AN EARLY AMBITION ⟪

Almost as soon as David could walk, soccer became an important part of his life. When he was three, he received a Manchester United outfit for Christmas. By that time, he was already in the habit of telling everyone, "I'm going to play soccer for Manchester United."

CROSS-CURRENTS

For some background on the pro soccer club that David dreaming of joining one day, read "Manchester United." Go to page 50. ▶▶

Of course, countless other boys throughout England were saying the same thing. But David was different. Drills in the backyard or the local park were a daily ritual for David and his dad. The practice was about fun, but it was also about building skills and learning to play the right way. David admits that sometimes he got frustrated with his father's emphasis on practice and technique. But he also acknowledges that without his father's training, he may never have become the player he is today.

When David turned seven, his father felt that he was good enough to begin **scrimmaging** with his club team. Ted made sure that no one cut the boy any slack:

> **❝If he'd been running around telling people not to tackle me all evening, it would have been pointless me being there in the first place. The fact that I always seemed to be playing soccer with players who were bigger and stronger than me when I was young, I'm sure, helped me later on in my career.❞**

This devotion to soccer was evident to everyone around him. A friend at Chase Lane Primary School, Matthew Treglohan, explained:

> **❝He was very good at art, but was only ever interested in football [soccer]. He wasn't even that bothered about girls then. A few of the kids shone through in football, but David was certainly one of the best.❞**

⇒ AN IMPORTANT AD ⇐

David soon proved his friend right. He hadn't yet turned eight when he saw an ad in the local paper: "WANTED: Football superstars of the future. Only talented boys need apply." David answered the ad and became a member of the Ridgeway Rovers. The team stayed together for several years, crossing the English Channel a number of times to play in tournaments in Europe.

When David was 11, he became the youngest-ever winner of the TSB Bobby Charlton Soccer Skills competition. Conducted by

Manchester United soccer legend Bobby Charlton, it was a week-long camp that fittingly took place at Old Trafford, the United field. He competed against players many years older than he was, including some who were in their late teens. As part of his prize, David got to go to Barcelona, Spain, and train for two weeks.

As an adult, Beckham fondly recalled the prestigious soccer school he attended before his teens. "As a young boy I attended the Bobby Charlton Soccer School with dreams of becoming a professional footballer," he said. "The experience changed my life, as I learnt from the best coaches and got to meet football heroes such as Bobby Charlton."

As a boy David dreamed of playing for Manchester United, a popular English football (soccer) club. Today, Manchester United remains one of the world's best-known sports teams—according to a 2007 survey, the club has more than 333 million fans worldwide. In this photo, the Manchester United squad is pictured during a match at the club's historic Old Trafford Stadium.

➤ A LOVE OF COOKING ➤

David's excellence in soccer didn't extend to his studies, however. More than one teacher described his performance in the classroom as "silly." But there was one class he enjoyed: home economics. As he explains in his autobiography:

> **"I enjoyed being in the kitchen when I was at home anyway. By the time I was thirteen, if Mum was working, she'd leave me to get dinner ready for all of us. If she was cutting hair at home, I'd make cups of tea and arrange little plates of biscuits for her clients while they were there at the house."**

This was an early indication of what would become one of David's defining characteristics: his interest in more "**feminine**" things, such as fashion, hairstyles, and skincare.

⋙ DAVID IS DISCOVERED ⋘

But years before the world ever came to know that side of him, David was busy playing for several teams and attracting the attention of scouts. One day his mother learned that a United scout had just seen one of his games. David later recalled:

> **❝I leaped into the air and started to cry. It was a dream come true. It was one of my best games for the district. Being from London and being a southerner, I never thought I would get seen by a scout of Man United.❞**

The scout had been impressed. The day David turned 13, he signed a schoolboy contract with the team of his dreams. As he said years later:

> **❝The day I signed didn't feel like the day I'd made it. The hard work was just starting. I wanted a challenge and Manchester United was the biggest challenge there was.❞**

David met all the challenges given to him. He starred on United's youth teams, helping them win the FA Youth Cup in 1992. He also made a few brief appearances with United itself as a midfielder.

In addition to skill, David also benefited from some good luck. At the end of the 1994–1995 season, United manager Alex Ferguson released several star players. Rather than replacing them with high-priced veterans, he gave several younger players a chance. David was one of them.

In August 1996, United was playing Wimbledon. It was David's second full season. One of his teammates slid him a short pass. What happened next has become legend.

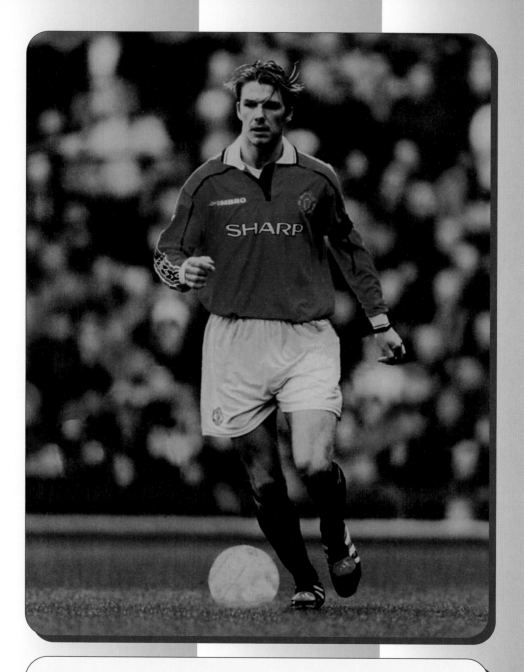

David controls the ball during a Manchester United game, 1996. It was that year—his second season with United—that David scored a famous goal against the Wimbledon team. His scoring helped the team win its second straight Premiere League title. As a result the Professional Footballers' Association named the 22-year-old "young player of the year."

3

Love, Fame, and Infamy

DAVID WAS STANDING UNGUARDED JUST INSIDE the midfield line. A quick glance downfield showed that the Wimbledon goalie was far in front of the goal. David thought to himself, "Why not? *Shoot*." As the ball rose high into the air, it appeared to be headed out of bounds beyond the left side of the goal.

But suddenly the ball bent back toward the goal. The goalie could do nothing as it dropped into the right corner of the goal. The television announcer shouted:

> **"That is absolutely phenomenal! David Beckham— surely an England player of the future—scores a goal that will be talked about and replayed for years!"**

The announcer was absolutely correct. As David explains in his autobiography:

> **"**[T]hat moment [in 1996] was the start of it all: the attention, the press coverage, the fame, that whole side of what's happened to me since. It changed forever that afternoon in South London, with one swing of a new boot. . . . When my foot struck that ball, it kicked open the door to the rest of my life at the same time.**"**

In particular, the goal attracted the notice of Glenn Hoddle, the English national team manager, who quickly added Beckham to the team. He played in his first **cap** a few weeks later.

SEEING HIS DREAM GIRL

Several months later, David was in a hotel room watching the Spice Girls on television. Their pictures were everywhere, and their music dominated the charts. David had developed a fondness for one of them—the posh one. He decided then and there that he would meet her, but he had no idea how.

A month later, David lucked out. Posh Spice (Victoria Adams) and Sporty Spice (Melanie Chisholm) attended a United game. Afterward, the two women came down to the players' lounge, along with their manager Simon Fuller.

David felt shy. Fuller introduced him to Victoria, but it didn't help. After a few awkward moments, the conversation ended, and Victoria walked away. It seemed David had missed his chance.

CROSS-CURRENTS
Read "The Spice Girls" if you'd like to learn more about one of the most successful pop music groups in history. Go to page 52. ▶▶

LIKING THE WAY HE LOOKED

However, there was still hope. As part of a magazine interview, the Spice Girls were photographed wearing soccer uniforms. Victoria wore a United jersey. According to the caption, she had chosen it because she liked the way David Beckham looked.

When Victoria came to David's next game, things between them went more smoothly. They began talking virtually nonstop. Soon afterward, they went out for dinner. The relationship moved quickly after that, though David needed a few dates to work up the courage to kiss her. Victoria said later that she fell in love with David in a matter of weeks after their first kiss.

"I started thinking about proposing a week after I met her," said David, about his relationship with Victoria "Posh Spice" Adams. The soccer star and the pop singer, pictured here in 2007, became inseparable during 1997. When Beckham proposed to Posh in January 1998, the news made newspaper headlines throughout the United Kingdom.

Things were going just as well on the field. David was named the Professional Footballers Association Young Player of the Year. He was also developing what would become his signature shot, the free kick. According to former United star Gordon Hill:

> **His toes are pointed downwards and away from him rather like a ballet dancer. But he keeps the ball on the inside of his foot . . . The fact his toes are pointed downward and away from him gives it that extra curve. There is no way a goalkeeper can stop it if it is struck properly.**

⇒ HIGH PHONE BILLS ⇐

The romance between David and Victoria also seemed unstoppable. There was only one problem: the Spice Girls were touring. The young couple spent a lot of time on the phone. According to David, the phone bills got quite scary, but they were the best investment he'd ever made. David proposed in January 1998, and Victoria accepted. Both were already so famous that news of the engagement made headlines throughout England.

Several months later, David was playing on the English team in the World Cup. Their opponent was Argentina, a somewhat bitter rival. Shortly before the game, Victoria called David from the United States—where she was on tour—with joyous news: She was pregnant! David was euphoric, but it didn't last long.

⇒ LAYING A TRAP ⇐

Early in the second half, with the score tied 2-2, Argentine captain Diego Simeone plowed into David from behind, flattening him. As David recounted in his autobiography:

> **"While I was down on the ground, he made as if to ruffle my hair. And gave it a tug. I flipped my leg up backwards towards him. It was instinctive, but the wrong thing to do. You just can't allow yourself to retaliate."**

Throwing his arms out to the side in the classic soccer gesture of a wounded player, Simeone tumbled to the ground. Afterward, he gloated that he had set up Beckham. The referee pulled out a yellow card, indicating a penalty for Simeone's foul. Then he held a red card aloft for David, which meant he was kicked out of the game.

⇒ ALL DAVID'S FAULT ⇐

CROSS-CURRENTS
To understand why British fans were so upset, read "The World Cup" for history of this important international soccer competition. Go to page 53. ▶▶

Now down a man, England was forced to play on the defensive. Regulation and extra time ended in a tie. The decision came down to penalty kicks. Argentina won, and David's countrymen blamed him for the defeat.

Dartboards with Beckham's face as the target spread throughout England. Burning Beckham **effigies** dangled from lampposts. He even had death threats.

David had only one way of replying: on the field. United had not done well the previous season, but he helped the team rebound and win The Treble: the Premier League championship, the Football Association Cup, and the European Champions Cup. In the Champions game, United trailed Germany's Bayern München 1-0.

Beckham (wearing the white uniform) challenges Ariel Ortega, a midfielder for the Argentine national team, during a 1998 World Cup second-round match. Beckham was later thrown out of the game for fouling Diego Simeone, the captain of Argentina's team. When England lost the match, Beckham was widely criticized by the national press and soccer fans.

In less than two minutes of **stoppage time**, United stormed back to win by converting a pair of Beckham's corner kicks into goals. David ended the year by being named runner-up to Rivaldo (of Brazil) for both European Player of the Year and FIFA Player of the Year.

➤ GETTING MARRIED ➤

Beckham's personal life was even better than his life on the field. In March 1999, Victoria gave birth to a boy they named Brooklyn, after the borough of New York City where Victoria had been when she called David with the news about her pregnancy. In honor of the event, David had his son's name tattooed on his lower back.

On July 4, 1999, the couple was married in a lavish ceremony at Luttrellstown Castle in Ireland. Soon afterward they bought a mansion outside London. It was quickly nicknamed "Beckingham Palace" as a takeoff on Buckingham Palace, the queen's official residence.

The following year David was named captain of the English national team. In 2001 he silenced any remaining hostility from 1998 when he curled in a penalty kick late in a World Cup qualifying game against Greece. It guaranteed England a place in the tournament the following year. At the end of the year, David was once again runner-up for FIFA Player of the Year honors.

The memory of the 1998 World Cup loss to Argentina was still fresh in David's mind as he prepared for the 2002 tournament. His eyes lit up when he saw the World Cup draw. There it was: June 7, 8:30 P.M., Sapporo, Japan—Argentina vs. England.

➤ LIFE'S OBSTACLES ➤

Even though David was looking forward to the rematch, he soon had much greater concerns than a soccer game. In February 2002, his parents announced their divorce. The news was devastating and may even have caused a string of poor performances on the field. To make matters worse, on April 10 David broke a bone in his foot when he was tackled hard by an Argentine player who had a reputation as a **hatchet man**.

In a huge irony, the movie *Bend It Like Beckham* was released less than 24 hours after the injury. The film had a feel-good ending. The real-life Beckham could only hope that his situation had a similar resolution.

CROSS-CURRENTS

For more information about the movie partly inspired by David's curving kicks, see "Bend It Like Beckham." Go to page 54. ▶▶

WORLD CUP SUPER GOALS

MONDAY, OCTOBER 8 2001

FREE WITH THE Sun

BECKHAM 7

SKIP, SKIP, HOORAY

DAVID BECKHAM, England's super skipper, jumps for joy as his injury-time goal against Greece puts England into the World Cup finals.

This insert from a British newspaper shows the crowd at Old Trafford Stadium cheering while Beckham celebrates his last-minute goal in the World Cup qualifying game against Greece, October 6, 2001. The game ended in a tie, which ensured that England's national team would earn a spot in the 2002 World Cup.

➤ THE CHANCE TO MAKE UP ➤

Though he wasn't at full strength, David's foot healed enough that he could play against Argentina in the World Cup. Just before the end of a scoreless first half, English star Michael Owen broke for the goal, and an Argentine defender tripped him. There was no doubt who would take the penalty kick.

As the referee spotted the ball, Simeone tried to play a mind game. He walked up to Beckham with his hand out. David ignored him.

He tried to settle himself by inhaling deeply. It didn't seem to help. The next moments are permanently written in his memory:

This photo captured David (red jersey) an instant before he launched a penalty kick toward the goal in the England-Argentina World Cup match on June 7, 2002, in Japan. The team captain booted the ball past the Argentine goaltender, and England won the match, 1-0. For Beckham, it was sweet revenge for his team's 1998 World Cup loss.

> **"I was far too nervous to try to be clever. Not nervous for myself any longer. This was all about the team I was captain of. I've never felt such pressure before. I ran forward. And I kicked the ball goalwards as hard as I could."**

⇒ "GOOOOOOAL!" ⇐

It went in. Flashbulbs exploded all over the stadium as David let out a huge roar. He rushed to the left corner of the field as several teammates swarmed over him. As *New York Times* writer George Vecsey noted:

> **David Beckham was releasing four years of emotion, four years of frustration. Rarely do you see a man exult and atone so publicly, so viscerally, but there he was, spiky hair and all, showing his teeth and flapping his red England jersey, in front of Argentina.**

It was the game's only goal. Though England lost to Brazil two weeks later in the quarterfinals, David had been redeemed. Less than three months later, he had even more to celebrate with the birth of his second son, Romeo. As with his first son, David had Romeo's name tattooed on his back. This time the mark was placed above the image of a guardian angel that he had inked across his shoulders and spine.

⇒ A WORRISOME PLOT ⇐

The joy turned to fear in November with the news that five men had been arrested for plotting to kidnap Victoria and the children and hold them for a ransom of £5 million (about $9.8 million in U.S. dollars). Though the plot was a hoax, the Beckhams installed extra security cameras and bought a bulletproof car. It was a clear sign of the downside of being famous.

As that memory faded and 2003 dawned, it seemed that David was living in a world that was virtually perfect. He seemed to have it all: fame, athletic prowess, a beautiful and loving wife, two very healthy children, and enough money to live very comfortably. What could possibly go wrong?

David Beckham is pictured with Alfredo di Stéfano, a legendary player and coach with the Spanish soccer club Real Madrid. In 2003 Beckham left Manchester United, signing a four-year contract to play for Real Madrid. He took jersey number 23 in honor of one of his heroes, basketball superstar Michael Jordan.

Hola, Señor Beckham

DURING THE EUPHORIA SURROUNDING MAN-
chester United's 1999 European Champions Cup
victory, David dedicated the win to Alex Ferguson.
Alex was the one who had given David a chance
and made his stunning career possible. According to
David, the team owed the manager everything. But
underneath the happiness there was tension between
the two men.

The United manager had been concerned about the effect of
all the off-field hoopla on David's career. He felt that David was
spending more time thinking about his family than about soccer.
The situation was like a powder keg, needing just a spark to set
it off.

In February 2003, Ferguson stormed into the United locker room
after a 2-0 loss. He lit into David, seemingly blaming him entirely
for the defeat. David swore back, and Ferguson became even more

furious. He kicked a soccer shoe lying on the floor. It struck David just above the left eye. David tried to charge Ferguson, but several teammates held him back. Though Ferguson quickly apologized, the incident became front-page news. David later realized that it marked the point of no return.

⇒ FOR SALE: DAVID BECKHAM ⇐

Three months later, United chief executive Peter Kenyon announced that if another team offered enough money, United would consider selling David. It was an uncomfortable situation. To get away from it all for awhile, David took his family on a vacation to the United States.

During the trip, David's agent called him to say that United had just posted a statement on the team's website. A team in Barcelona had made a conditional offer for him. If the conditions were met, the post continued, United would approve the sale.

David was floored. No one from the team had called him about the situation. In his autobiography, he wrote:

> **It was like they couldn't wait to get rid of me. I just sat down on the floor where I was. I was angry all right. I didn't like the news, and how I'd found out about it, some time after the rest of the world, was humiliating.**

⇒ A HARD GOODBYE ⇐

Beneath the anger was another feeling. The love affair that had begun while he was still a toddler and had endured for more than two decades was coming to an end.

> **For the first time, it was my relationship with the club that was slipping away. And that broke my heart. I had to start thinking seriously now about starting a career away from Old Trafford, after a lifetime of knowing that playing for United was all I'd ever wanted to do.**

But David had to be a realist. If he had to leave United, he didn't want to go to Barcelona. There was really only one team he wanted

Although Beckham was upset about leaving Manchester United, he was intrigued by the chance to play for a great Spanish team. Real Madrid had won the European club championship nine times in its history. One of these victories came the season before David arrived. The club featured many other talented players from around the world.

to play for: Real Madrid, a Spanish team. It had many of the same traditions as United and had been even more successful.

But the decision was still difficult. Leaving United meant uprooting his family, moving to a new country, and learning a new language and a new culture. He and Victoria were going on a trip to Japan, and they wanted things settled before they left. It came down to the wire.

They were in the airport when David's agent called with the news: Real Madrid had offered a four-year contract.

⋙ LIKE MICHAEL JORDAN ⋘

In Madrid, Beckham would be joining a team of soccer all-stars, led by three-time FIFA Player of the Year Zinedine Zidane. Because David's United jersey number, seven, belonged to another player, he took 23 in honor of basketball superstar Michael Jordan. Jordan is one of just a handful of athletes with whom Beckham could be regarded as a peer in terms of worldwide impact and recognition.

At about the same time, Beckham learned that Queen Elizabeth II had selected him to become an Officer of the Order of the British Empire. The OBE honors people for their contributions to society in fields such as politics, acting, music, and sports. David would receive his honor personally from the queen in November.

Although the plan to join the Madrid team seemed settled, there was a snag. Victoria didn't want to move to Madrid. She stayed at home in London. Then, a female assistant who went to Spain to help David claimed publicly that they had conducted a romantic affair. Though David denied it, the **alleged** affair quickly assumed front-page status. Things calmed down when Victoria finally agreed to move to Spain.

Even with his family situation resolved, and despite being surrounded with some of the greatest soccer talent in the world, David's time in Madrid was difficult. With his arrival, Real had been dubbed "Soccer's Dream Team." But while the team looked great on paper, it couldn't make the dream come true on the field. Even though David scored five times in his first 16 games and became a fan favorite, Real Madrid finished fourth at the end of his first year. The team had won La Liga, the top Spanish professional league, the year before David's arrival.

⋙ GIVING BACK ⋘

Though his career wasn't going quite the way he had wanted it to, David was becoming increasingly involved in charitable causes. He had already been associated with UNICEF—the United Nations Children's Fund—through Manchester United. Early in 2005, he was named a UNICEF Goodwill Ambassador, with special emphasis on alleviating the suffering caused by earthquake and **tsunami** in

David Beckham's signing with Real Madrid resulted in international media attention. His four-year deal with the Spanish club paid David about $7 million a season, plus bonuses. However, despite all the hype about Beckham's arrival, Real Madrid was unable to win a championship during his first few seasons with the club.

Indonesia. He made a TV commercial on behalf of UNICEF that was broadcast worldwide. He said:

> **"**It is one of the proudest moments of my life to be given the role of UNICEF Goodwill Ambassador and I hope to play a part in supporting these children at their time of need.**"**

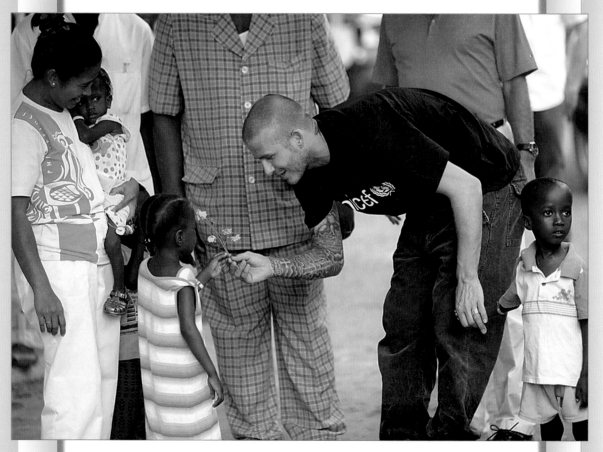

Five-year Senyo, who suffers from malnutrition, greets UNICEF Goodwill Ambassador David Beckham with yellow flowers upon his 2008 arrival at a feeding center in the town of Makeni, Sierra Leone, while Foday, who is also five and malnurished, holds David's hand. UNICEF provides money, food, medicine, and other supplies to help children and their families in poor countries around the world, and David is proud to be a Goodwill Ambassador.

David and Victoria welcomed their third son, Cruz David Beckham, on February 20. David marked the occasion by adding yet another tattoo. Since the birth of Brooklyn in 1999, he has gotten more than a dozen tattoos, all of which honor his family and their commitments to each other. Several include phrases in Hindi and Latin.

Soon after Cruz's birth, *People* magazine named David the World's Most Beautiful Sports Icon. In an interview, he acknowledged that Victoria had given him some tips that helped him achieve the honor.

> **"Being out in the cold and rain doesn't help your skin, so moisturiser in the morning is a big thing. And at night it's the eye cream. A manicure is probably my favourite pampering splurge."**

⟫ THE OLYMPICS FOR LONDON ⟪

In 2005 Beckham became one of the highest-profile supporters of London's bid to host the 2012 Olympic Games. In May he traveled to Singapore with Prime Minister Tony Blair and two-time Olympic gold medal winner Sebastian Coe, the organizing committee's chairman, in an appeal to the International Olympic Committee. The proposed site of the Games made it easy for him to become an advocate.

> **"For me, there's only one place that this Olympics could be and that's in the East End of London. One, because I grew up there; two, because I realise how inspiring the East End can be; and three, the biggest thing for me in the East End is the passion."**

While it's impossible to determine how effective his words were, they certainly didn't hurt. London won the bid.

That fall, David opened the first David Beckham Soccer Academies, in London and Los Angeles. He was very clear about his objective in establishing them:

> **"It's about kids coming down, getting off the streets, having fun. If we find great new talent, then that's good. But the most important thing is the kids coming down. They're learning about football, they're learning about their body and injuries that you can get. And, also, they're having fun."**

Victoria and David pose for a photo at the opening of a David Beckham Academy in Los Angeles, June 2005. This was their second soccer school. The first had been opened a few months earlier in East London, near David's childhood home. At the time, David said that he hoped the schools would help young players.

⇶ MAKING HISTORY ⇶

Beckham and Real Madrid were unable to win the La Liga championship for the next few seasons. But David's disappointing performances in Spain were partially overshadowed by his accomplishments in the 2006 World Cup. He was captain of England's national team, though this time there was no England-Argentina drama. Instead, David made history when he became the first English player to score in three successive World Cups.

David stepped down as captain after England was eliminated in the quarterfinals. At a press conference, he said:

> **"I feel the time is right to pass on the armband [the symbol of being captain] as we enter a new era under new coach Steve McClaren . . . It has been an honour . . . and I want to stress that I wish to continue to play for England and look forward to helping . . . in any way I can."**

Later in 2006, the Beckhams revealed that Romeo suffered from epilepsy. The disease is characterized by sudden seizures, which can be triggered by many things, including flashing lights. Victoria pleaded with paparazzi not to take photos of the toddler, as a constant barrage of flashes could easily cause a seizure.

≫ A NEAT FREAK ≪

It wasn't the only time that the family spoke about its health problems. In a television interview in late March, David revealed that he suffered from obsessive-compulsive disorder. He also managed to get in a plug for one of his primary sponsors:

> **"I have got this obsessive-compulsive disorder where I have to have everything in a straight line or everything has to be in pairs. I'll put my Pepsi cans in the fridge and if there's one too many then I'll put it in another cupboard somewhere."**

CROSS-CURRENTS

If you would like to better understand how David's psychological disorder affects his life, read "Obsessive-Compulsive Disorder." Go to page 55. ▶▶

In the summer of 2006, David felt that he was in a cupboard himself. Fabio Capello, one of the world's most successful soccer managers, took over Real Madrid in an effort to improve its league standing. Despite fan protests, he quickly relegated David to the sidelines.

The move soon became part of a double whammy. In mid-August, Steve McClaren revealed that his new era for the English national team wouldn't include David. It was a painful blow.

DAVID BECKHAM

David enjoys spending time with his children. He was photographed with sons Brooklyn and Romeo at an outside event in Beverly Hills. The Beckhams have a third son, Cruz, who was born in February 2005. Friends of the Beckham family have said that Victoria and David would like to have more children someday.

Because of his international fame, many companies have asked David Beckham to promote their products. In 2007, for example, the David Beckham Academy signed a deal to promote a nutritional supplement for children made by the European corporation Findus. However, not all of the products that David has promoted have been successful.

And it wasn't the last disappointment. A line of fragrances David and Victoria launched in the fall didn't sell as well as expected. Additionally, one of his sponsors, Police Sunglasses, replaced him as spokesman with actor Antonio Banderas. With all the bad news coming in, David and Victoria began considering their alternatives. More and more it appeared that their future—in particular David's playing career—could benefit from a change of scenery.

Beckham handles the ball during a game for the Los Angeles Galaxy. The English soccer superstar made headlines around the world when he decided to bring his skills to America in 2007. When Beckham's deal with the Galaxy was announced, Major League Soccer (MLS) clubs saw an immediate increase in fan interest.

5

Coming to America

THE BECKHAMS SOON CAME TO A DECISION about David's future. Though Real Madrid offered David a contract extension, he decided to sign with the Los Angeles Galaxy in 2007. He had already played for two of the biggest soccer clubs in the world and spent 15 years competing at the highest level. It was time for a new challenge.

The announcement set off shock waves throughout the United States, where the size of his contract rivaled those of top professional athletes in major American sports. Christine Brennan of *USA Today* summed it up:

> **David Beckham coming to the United States is . . . [like] Tiger Woods meeting Brad Pitt on the red carpet. This transcends sports. This is a big, big deal.**

But not everyone was as impressed, especially in England where the MLS is not regarded very highly. Many English fans felt that David was "rubbish." Only players who were washed up would go to play soccer in the United States, they said.

⇛ NOTHING BUT NET ⇚

Early in 2007, David also made a commitment to support a charitable organization called **Malaria** No More. The charity seeks to increase public awareness of the disease—one of the world's deadliest—and raise money to combat it. According to the National Institutes of Health, 300 to 500 million cases of malaria occur each year, and more than one million people die annually from the disease.

As spokesman, David focused on one particular aspect of Malaria No More's campaign: mosquito netting. A $10 donation would purchase a bed net. Those nets are used to shelter mothers and their infants while they sleep at night, the time when the mosquitoes that carry the disease are most active. He recorded a public service announcement featuring the netting used for soccer goals. "We need nets" appears at the end of the spot, followed by "Mosquito nets could stop 3000 African children dying every day."

⇛ COMING AROUND ⇚

David was still under contract with Real Madrid when he signed with the Galaxy, so he couldn't report to his new team right away. His contract did not start until July 1, 2007. Meanwhile in Spain, Real was continuing to struggle, and manager Fabio Capello decided to put David back on the field.

That wasn't Beckham's only reversal of fortune. In May, McClaren had a change of heart and invited David to play on the English national team. David justified McClaren's decision by assisting on a goal in a 1-1 tie with Brazil.

Real Madrid similarly rallied with Beckham back on the team. They won the La Liga title with a victory on the final day of the season in mid-June. David had finally won the championship that had been so widely expected when he joined the team four years earlier. Unfortunately, David injured his ankle during the game. It still hadn't healed when he joined the Galaxy the following month.

Flanked by players for the Chicago Fire, David (center, white uniform) battles for the ball, October 21, 2007. The game ended in a 1-0 defeat for the Galaxy, ensuring that Los Angeles would miss the MLS playoffs. In David's first season, the Galaxy finished with a disappointing record of nine wins, 14 losses, and seven ties.

⇒ Not What He Planned ⇐

When David joined his new team in the United States, his injured ankle continued to hamper him. He scored his first goal for the Galaxy in August, but he suffered a knee injury soon afterward and played in only two more games. Clearly it wasn't the kind of performance he had envisioned back in January. The Galaxy finished with the third-worst record in the league. David told *60 Minutes* that it was a nightmare.

To MLS officials, however, his arrival was a dream come true. Overall game attendance shot up more than 50 percent after David joined the Galaxy. The MLS website nearly doubled its total number of hits. Television ratings increased significantly. And "Beckham" number 23 jerseys increased soccer apparel sales a phenomenal 780 percent. League officials maintain that his jersey is now the best-selling single player shirt worldwide. So it was no wonder that following the conclusion of the season, MLS commissioner Don Garber said:

> **❝The signing of David Beckham delivered on our expectations on every measure. He certainly raises our awareness and credibility here and abroad. The interest in our league in England is off the charts. Before David Beckham, we weren't covered on the BBC.❞**

David was also receiving plenty of coverage on the BBC himself as he continued to play on the English national team. In late November, he played in his 99th cap. He seemed destined to become just the fifth English player to reach the century mark. However, McClaren was dismissed soon after David's 99th game. Fabio Capello—who had been fired by Real Madrid in spite of winning La Liga—signed as his replacement. David's status was again uncertain. Capello's responsibility was to win games, and it was up to him to choose the players he felt would best achieve that goal.

⇛ West Africa's Children ⇜

None of the ups and downs in his career kept David from his charitable work. In January, he traveled to the African nation of Sierra Leone in his role as UNICEF Goodwill Ambassador. He put the issue of child survival in the spotlight. One of four children in Sierra Leone won't reach the age of five, the highest under-five mortality rate in the world. He visited clinics and gave medicine to ill children.

> **❝We can't turn a blind eye to tens of thousands of young children who die every day in the developing world, mostly from causes that are preventable. It's**

shocking and tragic, especially when the solutions are simple—things like vaccinations against measles or using a mosquito net to reduce the chance of getting malaria.**"**

Not everything about his visit was serious, though. At one point, he passed a group of young men playing soccer. He quickly turned his car around, hopped out, and joined the game. The men quickly recognized him, chanting his name and rubbing his head.

While visiting Freetown, the capital of Sierra Leone, David spotted a roadside soccer game and joined the young players, January 2008. Beckham was visiting the war-torn African country in his role as a UNICEF Goodwill Ambassador. His goal was to direct international attention to the problems of children in countries like Sierra Leone.

When David returned from Africa, Capello still hadn't indicated whether he would play when England hosted Switzerland on February 6. Both Alex Ferguson and former national team manager Sven Goran Eriksson—under whom David had played 62 caps—urged Capello to put him on the roster. Despite the support, though, in an interview Eriksson seemed to echo the **disdain** about the quality of play in the MLS:

The 2008 season turned out to be a good one for David Beckham. In addition to playing well with the Galaxy—he is pictured here in a preseason game against a Japanese club—David was asked to serve again as captain of England's national team for a June match against Trinidad and Tobago.

> **"**I don't want to interfere with Fabio Capello's job, but I believe David deserves to be in the team. Not just because it will be his 100th cap, but because he's still a great player. His right foot is as good as ever. Even if he is now playing in America, David can still fight for his place.**"**

➤ OUT OF SHAPE ➤

Capello soon made his decision. David wouldn't play. The primary reason, he said, was that David wasn't in game shape. He had a point. Even though David had been training hard with the Arsenal team in Holloway, North London, he had also spent considerable time jetting around the world. Antarctica was the only continent where he hadn't set foot. While some of these trips involved exhibition games with the Galaxy, others were charitable and did not involve training. One such trip was to Brazil to announce the opening of his third soccer academy, in the coastal resort town of Natal.

David admitted that Capello's judgment had been correct. His conditioning hadn't been good enough to play against Switzerland. But several exhibitions in Asia with the Galaxy during his world tour had changed that. Once David was back in top form, Capello added him back to the English team. He would be facing France in late March for his 100th cap. When he heard the news, he said:

> **"**I'm honored that I'm making, hopefully, my 100th appearance in an England shirt, but I'm also honored to be doing it against one of the best teams in the world.**"**

While playing in the game with France was certainly a highlight moment for David, it didn't rank among his top performances. David picked up a yellow card late in the first half, and Capello substituted for him at the 62-minute mark. The manager, however, made it clear that pulling him from the game had nothing to do with how he was playing. He simply wanted to have an extended look at David's replacement. Even after being replaced, David's spirits were high.

❝I'm very honored. Straight from when I started playing for England I never dreamed I'd get 100 caps, and hopefully beyond. I'm happy but like I said during the week I want to carry on.❞

⟫ DAVID'S SECOND SEASON BEGINS ⟪

His desire to "carry on" was a clear reference to the 2010 World Cup, which will be held in South Africa. In the meantime, there was the MLS season, which began on March 29, 2008, just three days after

Many people had high hopes when David—pictured here with young fans—joined the Los Angeles Galaxy. "David Beckham is a global sports icon," said MLS Commissioner Don Garber when the superstar joined the league. "[His] enormous success as a player and team leader will serve as an inspiration to millions of soccer players and fans in this country."

the match against France. The Galaxy's first match was against the Colorado Rapids.

Though the Galaxy was hammered, 4-0, in their opening game against the Rapids, they rebounded in their home debut before a capacity crowd on April 3. David scored the opening goal and assisted on the other in a 2-0 victory. The victory seemed to bear out his words a few days earlier about the prospects for the season:

> **"It was difficult last season because I came half-way through and wasn't fit. Touch wood, the ankle's good, the knee's good. I'm definitely prepared physically and mentally, and definitely ready for the upcoming season."**

Should David's good health continue for the rest of the season, there can be little doubt that it would go a long way toward increasing the popularity of soccer in the United States.

Though David Beckham is relatively old for a world-class soccer player, in other respects he is still a young man. When he retires from the field, he will have opportunities to continue making a difference in the world around him. Many people believe that these opportunities will include a knighthood, especially since two of the four other soccer players to reach the 100-cap mark—Bobby Moore and Bobby Charlton—have received that honor.

Soccer has given David much to be thankful for. Now he hopes that he can give back. His goal? To show the world's most powerful nation what the world's most popular sport is all about.

CROSS-CURRENTS

Read "Modern-day Knights" to learn how the most influential British athletes and entertainers are knighted in recognition of their accomplishments. Go to page 55. ▶▶

Major League Soccer

Major League Soccer (MLS) was formed as part of a deal that granted the United States the bid to host the World Cup in 1994. The league began play in 1996 with 10 teams: the Columbus Crew, D.C. United, New England Revolution, New York/New Jersey MetroStars, Tampa Bay Mutiny, Colorado Rapids, Dallas Burn, Kansas City Wiz, Los Angeles Galaxy, and San Jose Clash (later Earthquakes).

After the first year, attendance began to decline. Nevertheless, the league expanded to 12 teams in 1998, though it fell back to 10 three years later. The strong showing of the U.S. team in the 2002 World Cup led to an increase in interest in the league. Two years later, it began adding teams again. The 2008 season began with 14 teams, and the league anticipates adding four more by 2012.

The league is divided into Eastern and Western Conferences. Teams play 30 games in the regular season that begins in late March and ends at the end of October. Eight teams qualify for the playoffs, with the championship game in late November. (Go back to page 6.)

Pelé

Edison Arantes do Nascimento was born into poverty in a small town in Brazil in 1940. He was named for the famous American inventor Thomas Edison, but acquired his better-known nickname at a fairly early age. He disliked the name Pelé intensely, but the more he protested, the more the name stuck.

Pelé came by his interest in soccer naturally. His father was a professional soccer player whose career was cut short due to a knee injury. Pelé's talent was obvious at an early age, and he was signed to a professional contract with the Santos team when he was 15.

He played in his first World Cup in 1958, and at just 17, he was the youngest player in Cup history. He scored twice in the final game, and Brazil won the trophy. Four years later he suffered an injury early on in the tournament, although Brazil went on to claim the trophy again.

A Historic First

In 1966 Pelé became the first player to score a goal in three successive World Cups. But in an opening round match against Portugal, he was tackled especially hard and was forced to leave the game. Brazil was quickly eliminated, and Pelé said he would not play in any future World Cups.

By then, however, his worldwide reputation had soared. Despite his earlier declaration, he agreed to play for Brazil in the 1970 World Cup. He had a hand in most of his team's goals, and Brazil won again. It was his last international match.

A Memorable Finale

The New York Cosmos signed Pelé in 1974 to increase interest in the North American Soccer League (NASL). In 1977 he led the Cosmos to the NASL title. Later that year, Pelé closed out his career in an **exhibition match** between the Cosmos and Santos. Before a packed stadium and a worldwide television audience, he played one half for each team and scored his final goal.

In 1999 Pelé was named the Athlete of the Century by the International Olympic Committee. The following year he was voted Footballer of the Century by the Fédération Internationale de Football Association, the sport's governing body. *Time* magazine honored him even

Brazilian soccer star Pelé was expected to attract new American fans to soccer when he agreed to play for the New York Cosmos in the mid-1970s. (A headline on this June 1975 issue of Sports Illustrated declares "U.S. Soccer Finds a Savior.") During his three years with the Cosmos, Pelé did raise interest in the sport among young Americans.

further by naming him one of the Time 100, the most important people of the twentieth century. (Go back to page 8.) ◀◀

Manchester United

The famous English soccer club Manchester United originated in 1878. The club was formed by a group of Manchester workers on the Lancashire and Yorkshire Railway, who wanted something to do on their free Saturday afternoons. They each chipped in to buy balls and other gear and formed the Newton Heath L&YR (Lancashire and Yorkshire Railway) Football Club. They were soon beating all the other local teams, in part because talented out-of-towners would join Newton Heath L&YR in order to get good-paying jobs on the railroad.

The team nearly went bankrupt at the turn of the century, but J.H. Davies of Manchester Breweries gave it enough cash to continue. To reflect their new start, the name was changed to Manchester United in 1902. Eight years later, the club's new facility—Old Trafford—was completed. A newspaper writer of the time praised the stadium:

> **"As a football ground it is unrivalled in the world, it is an honour to Manchester and the home of a team who can do wonders when they are so disposed."**

Decline and Recovery

At first the team lived up to the expectations the stadium created, but soon United fell into a long decline. Additionally, Old Trafford stadium was damaged during World War II. It was eventually rebuilt, and likewise the team began doing better.

But in 1958 tragedy struck. An airplane crash during a refueling stop in Munich, Germany, killed or crippled more than half the team members and other key personnel. Many people expected United to fold, but the team struggled on. Within a decade, players such as George Best and Bobby Charlton (who would eventually be knighted for his achievements) elevated Manchester United to the top rank of English soccer.

Enter Alex Ferguson

United faded again during the 1970s and 1980s but recovered after Alex Ferguson was appointed as manager. His confidence in grooming young players such as David proved to be justified. The team won 17 major trophies in 17 years. In 1999 United accomplished a feat called The Treble, by winning three major championships in the same year. They became the first English team to win The Treble. The team continued to play well following that dream season and was considered among the most valuable athletic franchises anywhere in the world. In 2005 American businessman Malcolm Glazer bought the team for more than $1.6 billion.

(Go back to page 12.)

Alex Ferguson has served as the manager of Manchester United since 1986. He has won more trophies than any other manager in the history of English soccer. When United lost several stars after the 1994 season, Ferguson was criticized for replacing them with young players—including 22-year-old David Beckham. The young stars quickly led United to a pair of championships.

The Spice Girls

The Spice Girls were formed in 1994 by music industry managers Chris and Bob Herbert. They saw how successful "boy bands" had become, and thought that an all-girl group could be equally big. The group consisted of five young singer/dancers, all with Spice nicknames: Baby Spice (Emma Bunton), Ginger Spice (Geri Halliwell), Posh Spice (Victoria Adams), Scary Spice (Melanie Brown), and Sporty Spice (Melanie Chisholm).

The group signed a deal with English talent manager Simon Fuller in 1995, and released "Wannabe," their first single, the following year. It was an immediate hit, eventually topping the charts in more than 30 countries and becoming the all-time best-selling single by an all-girl group. Their first two albums, *Spice* (1996) and *Spiceworld* (1997), sold so many copies and generated so much excitement that the Spice Girls were compared favorably with the Beatles. *Spiceworld: The Movie*, released in late 1997, featured many well-known actors and grossed more than $100 million.

After a world tour early in 1998, Geri left the group. The other four continued performing together for several years, though they began pursuing solo careers in 2001. All five returned for a reunion tour in December 2007 that created an almost unprecedented ticket demand. (Go back to page 18.) ◀◀

During the mid-1990s, the Spice Girls—(from left) Sporty (Melanie Chisholm), Baby (Emma Bunton), Scary (Melanie Brown), Ginger (Geri Halliwell), and Posh (Victoria Adams)— became international stars almost overnight, selling millions of albums. Although each of the Spice Girls had started solo careers by 2001, the group reunited for a concert tour during 2007 and 2008.

The World Cup

Next to the Olympic Games, the World Cup is probably the world's most popular sports event. Held every four years, it consists of a tournament among 32 national soccer teams. Only the host nation is guaranteed a chance to play. The remaining 31 teams are determined by qualifying tournaments that begin much earlier.

The tournament begins with a group stage. The teams are divided into eight groups of four teams each. The teams in each group play a round-robin format. The winner of each match receives three points, while both teams collect one point in tie games.

The two teams in each group with the most points advance to the knockout stage. Here, the winners of each group play the second place team from another group. Matches are played until a single winner is determined. The final match is among the world's highest-viewed sports programs. It is estimated that more than 700 million people watched the 2006 final between France and Italy.

Since the first World Cup tournament was held in 1930, only seven different national teams have won the title. Brazil has won the World Cup five times, while Italy has won four and Germany has won three times. The national teams of Uruguay and Argentina have each won the title twice, while England and France have each won the World Cup once. England's victory came in 1966, nearly a decade before David Beckham was born.

Although the United States placed third in the first tournament in 1930, no U.S. team has ever equaled that achievement. The U.S. team beat England 1-0 in 1950 in the group stage in one of the tournament's greatest upsets, but didn't advance. It would be four decades before another American team qualified for the World Cup, but the 1990 team went 0-3 in the group stage.

It was a different story in 1994 when the United States hosted the World Cup. The team tied its first match, then faced Colombia, the fourth-ranked team in the world. Aided by an **own goal** by a Colombian player (who was murdered when he returned home), the U.S. squad pulled out a 2-1 win and advanced to the knockout stage. There, they lost 1-0 to Brazil.

The U.S. rebounded in 2002. The team reached the knockout stage, defeated Mexico, and advanced to the quarter-finals. But they lost 1-0 to Germany. The momentum didn't carry over to 2006, however, as the U.S. team did not make it out of the group stage.

(Go back to page 20.)

Bend It Like Beckham

The 2002 film *Bend It Like Beckham* revolves around Jessminder (Jess), a teenaged British Indian girl who wants to play soccer even though her traditional parents oppose it. They want her to act like her older sister by finding a good Indian boy and marrying him.

Jess, who has papered the walls of her bedroom with David Beckham posters, would much rather sneak out and play every chance she gets. Soon she meets Jules, a white girl who has her own set of parental issues. Jules belongs to an organized team and invites Jess to join them. Jess has to spin an increasingly complex set of lies in order to keep playing. The situation comes to a head when her sister's wedding falls on the same day as an important tournament.

When David and Victoria saw an early screening of the movie, they liked it so much that they offered to play themselves in bit roles. However, the plan fell through because their schedules were so hectic. The director had to use lookalikes, instead.

The movie was a surprise hit. It was also the first major role for Keira Knightley, who used her performance as Jules as a springboard to star in the blockbuster *Pirates of the Caribbean: The Curse of the Black Pearl.*

(Go back to page 22.)

Jess (played by Parminder Nagra) speaks with her coach, Joe (Jonathan Rhys-Meyers) in a scene from Bend it Like Beckham. *The 2002 movie won several awards, received good reviews from movie critics, and was the top-earning British film of the year. One of Victoria Beckham's songs, "IOU," was included on the film's soundtrack.*